Time-Travel Guides

The Shang Dynasty

Tim Cooke

Gareth Stevens Publishing

Please visit our website, www.garethstevens.com. For a free color catalog of all our high-quality books, call toll free 1-800-542-2595 or fax 1-877-542-2596.

Cataloging-in-Publication Data

Names: Cooke, Tim, 1961-, author.
Title: The Shang dynasty / Tim Cooke.
Description: Buffalo, NY : Gareth Stevens Publishing, 2026. |
Series: Time-travel guides | Includes glossary and index.
Identifiers: ISBN 9781482475487 (pbk.) | ISBN 9781482475494 (library bound) |
ISBN 9781482475500 (ebook)
Subjects: LCSH: China--History--Shang dynasty, 1766-1122 B.C.--Juvenile literature.
Classification: LCC DS744.C67 2026 | DDC 931'.02--dc23

Published in 2026 by
Gareth Stevens Publishing
2544 Clinton St.
Buffalo, NY 14224

First published in Great Britain in 2022 by Hodder & Stoughton

Artwork and Design: Collaborate Agency
Editor: Sarah Silver

Picture credits:
p.4-5: © johnbraid/Shutterstock.com, p.28: © Vincenzo Iacovoni/Shutterstock.com,

Printed in China
CPSIA compliance information: Batch #QW26GS: For further information contact Gareth Stevens at 1-800-542-2595.

CONTENTS

YIN

Welcome to Yin! This is the capital city of the Shang, the first dynasty that archaeologists are certain ruled part of ancient China. (A dynasty is a series of rulers that belonged to the same family.) The Shang controlled a large area of the Huang He (Yellow River) valley from about 1600 BCE to 1046 BCE. You can use time-traveling technology to go back to discover more about the city and the people who lived there.

Guesswork

For centuries, people told stories about the Shang, but there was no evidence of them. Some experts believed the Shang never actually existed! That all changed when the ruins of Yin were discovered in the 1920s (see page 29).

TIME-TRAVEL GUIDES

Your time-travel guide

Congratulations for buying this Time-Travel Guidebook – the must-have companion for travelers journeying into the past. This guidebook will give you expert advice on where to stay, what to see, and how best to spend your time in Yin. Top travel tips throughout will tell you what to bring, where to shop, and what to look out for.

This photo shows the modern entrance to Yin and a reconstruction of some buildings. Very little of the original city remains – just a few earthworks and tombs.

Lots of names!

The Shang capital has had several names, so don't get confused. Today it is called Yinxu or Anyang. In the past, it was also called Xiaotun. But at the time when we're visiting, at the peak of Shang power, it is called Yin.

Top Tip

What to pack

Bring your own chopsticks if you don't want to eat with your hands. The Shang use bronze chopsticks for cooking – but not for eating. When eating, you'll tear meat apart with your fingers and scoop up rice and soup with the palms of your hands. It can get messy!

Look out for: turtles and oxen

The Shang believed they could predict the future by using oracle bones (see pages 12–13). These were made from turtle shells and ox bones. Expect to see lots of both those animals.

PUTTING YIN ON THE MAP

Yin is the last Shang capital – and the most important. Before moving here, the Shang had five other capitals, all on the North China Plain, close to the Huang He (Yellow River). Nobody really knows why the Shang moved their capital city so often. King Pan Geng moved his court here around 1400 BCE, where they settled close to the Huan (or Anyang) River.

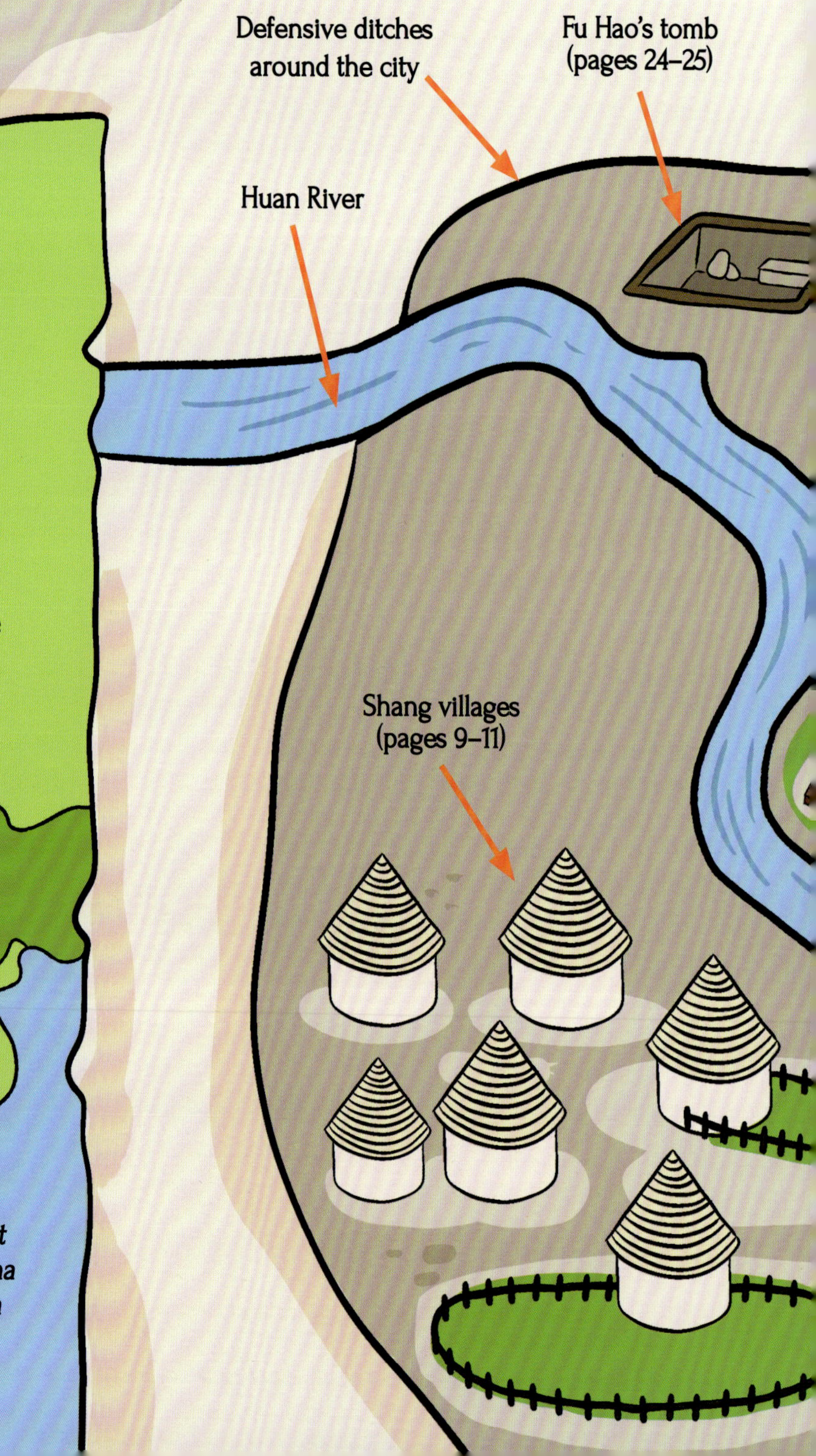

The Shang's neighbors

The Shang's neighbors, the Sanxingdui, lived near the Yangtze River, about 14 miles (23 km) from modern-day Chengdu in Sichuan Province. Like the Shang, the Sanxingdui were experts at using metal, such as bronze and gold. More than 13,000 objects have been found at a Sanxingdui site. There's clearly more to learn about the Shang's mysterious neighbors!

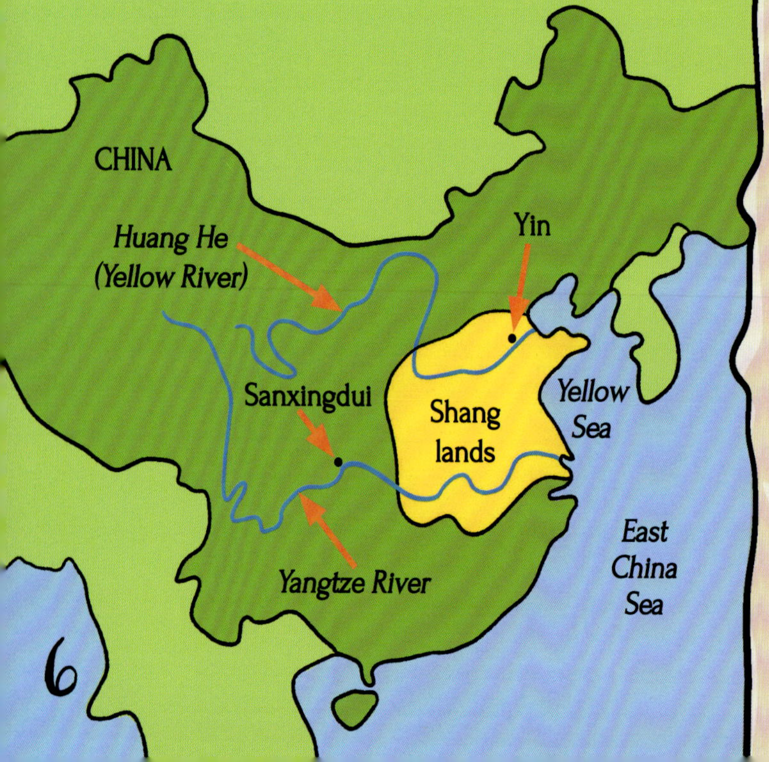

Top Tip

Be careful where you go

Shang society is very exclusive. Ordinary people cannot go into royal buildings uninvited. Only nobles and officials can go there – together with the royal family, of course. Don't worry. If you're lucky and meet someone important enough, they may be able to get you an invitation to the best places!

Look out for: tombs

To the west of the palace, see if you can spot the tombs, where important men and women, such as Fu Hao (left) were buried.

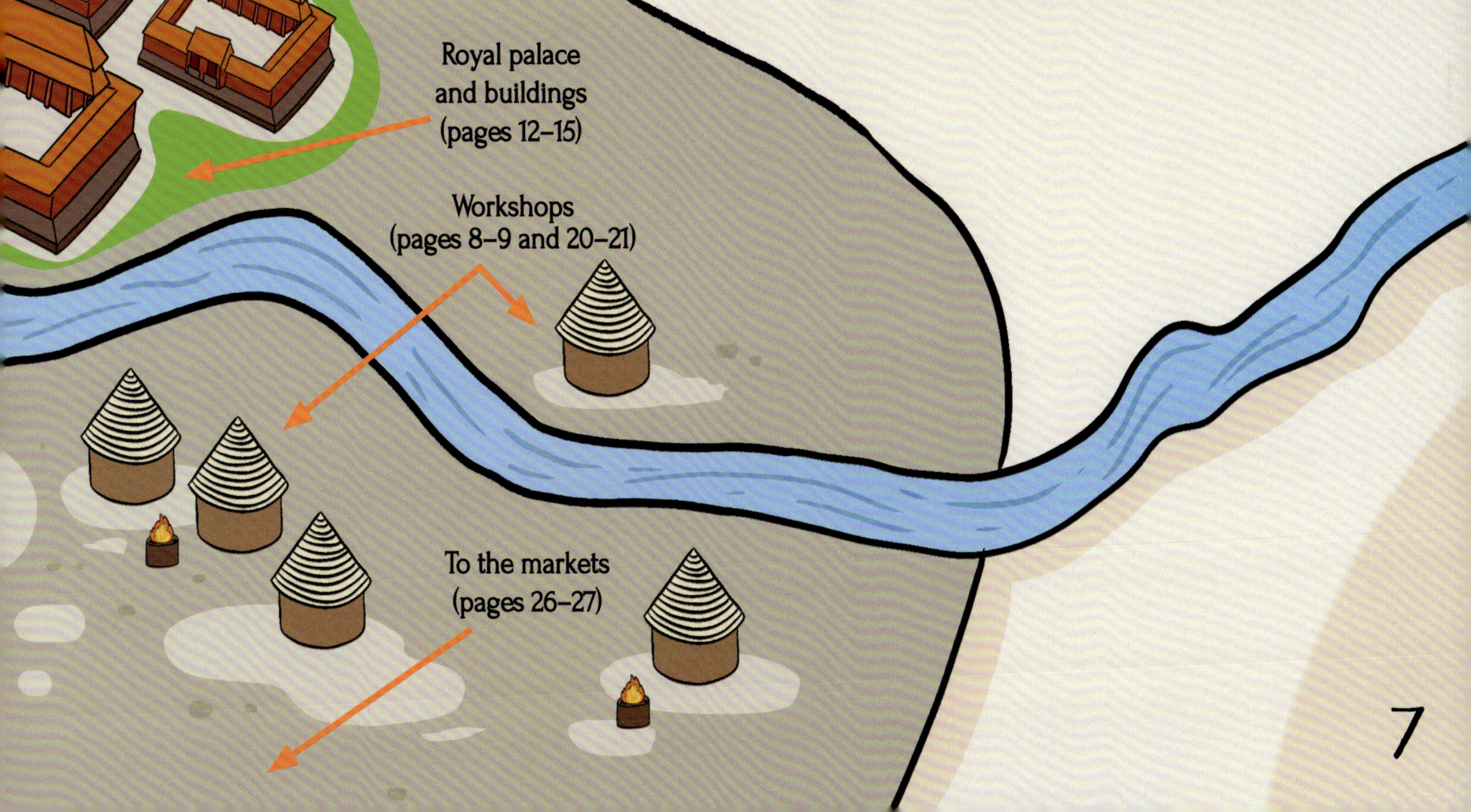

MEET THE PEOPLE

Take a stroll around Yin's city streets. You're likely to meet all sorts of interesting people, including craftspeople, merchants, and some armed warriors. You'll see enslaved people too. Many were captured during wars with the Shang's neighbors.

Meet the makers

Shang craftspeople are very important. Some are highly skilled bronze workers. At workshops you can see how weapons, including swords and axes, are made. Bronze workers also make vessels and bells in complicated shapes. Jewelry is very popular too, so look out for people making rings, necklaces, and other items. The Shang love bling!

A new friend

On your first day in the city, a craftsman comes out of his workshop to greet you. He's fascinated because he's never met a time traveler before. He invites you to stay with his family. He'll be happy to answer any questions you might have. Even better, he's such an important craftsman that he can get you into parts of the royal palace.

Top Tip

Get outside the city

If possible, try to visit some farms and farmers outside the city. You'll get a better idea of what life is like for most Shang people.

Meet the farmers

Most ordinary Shang people work as farmers, but you won't really see them in the city. They live in villages and work in the fields on the edge of Yin. Farmers grow enough food for everyone. They have to give most of what they grow to the king, who owns all the land. The king makes sure everyone has enough to eat. That helps ensure that everyone is happy to have him as their ruler.

WHERE TO STAY

Shang homes aren't luxurious, but you'll still be comfortable. Like most Shang people, your host lives in a circular home dug into the ground, with a fireplace in the middle. It has a roof of thatch with a hole to let out any smoke. Being partly buried helps the houses stay warm in the winter and cool in the summer.

Rammed earth

The walls of Shang palaces, temples, and homes are all made from the same material: earth! Builders construct frames and then pack them full of earth. They ram it down and down to knock all the air out of it. The earth eventually becomes as hard as stone, so the frames can be removed.

In ordinary homes, a thatched roof rests on top of the walls. In bigger buildings, such as palaces and temples, the thatched roof is held up by wooden pillars.

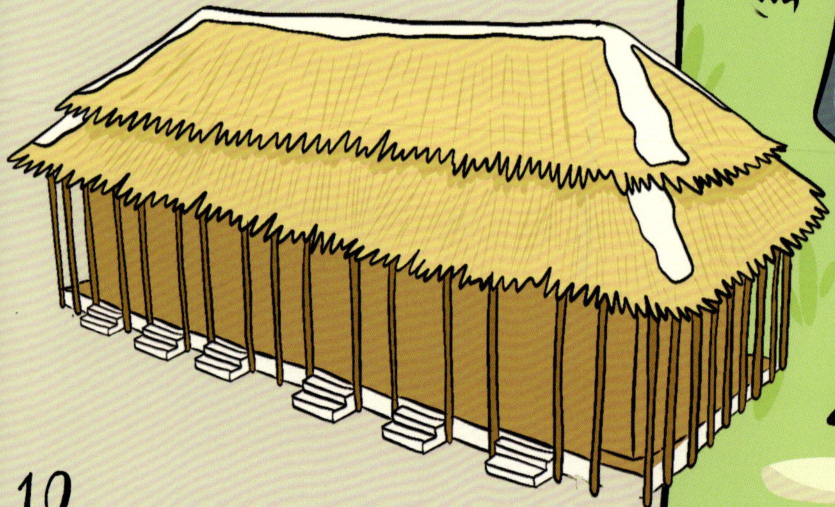

Sleeping and eating

When you visit your host's home, you'll discover that the whole family lives and sleeps in the same room. This is how everyone lives. Most homes have very little furniture. People sleep on raised wooden platforms, and there is a special area for eating.

Look out for: pottery cups

As a time traveler , you will most likely eat and drink from bowls and cups made from wood or pottery, like ordinary Shang people do. Pottery smashes easily, so a lot of this everyday crockery survives today only as lots of tiny pieces.

LEARN THE FUTURE

If you get the chance to walk among the palace buildings, be sure to take it! Don't be surprised to see pools full of turtles. These animals play a very important part in Shang religion.

Look out for: oracle bones

Oracle bones are either made from the flat bottoms of turtle shells or the shoulder bones of oxen. The priests write down questions for the god Shang Di (see page 14) on the bones. Other priests heat the bones in flames until they crack. Special priests, called diviners, "read" the cracks and announce what they believe to be Shang Di's answer. The king then follows this advice.

Top Tip

Writing

The writing on oracle bones might look familiar. That's because the Shang created the first system of Chinese writing. Shang writing was adopted by the later Qin Dynasty (221–206 BCE). It became the foundation of the writing system still used in China today.

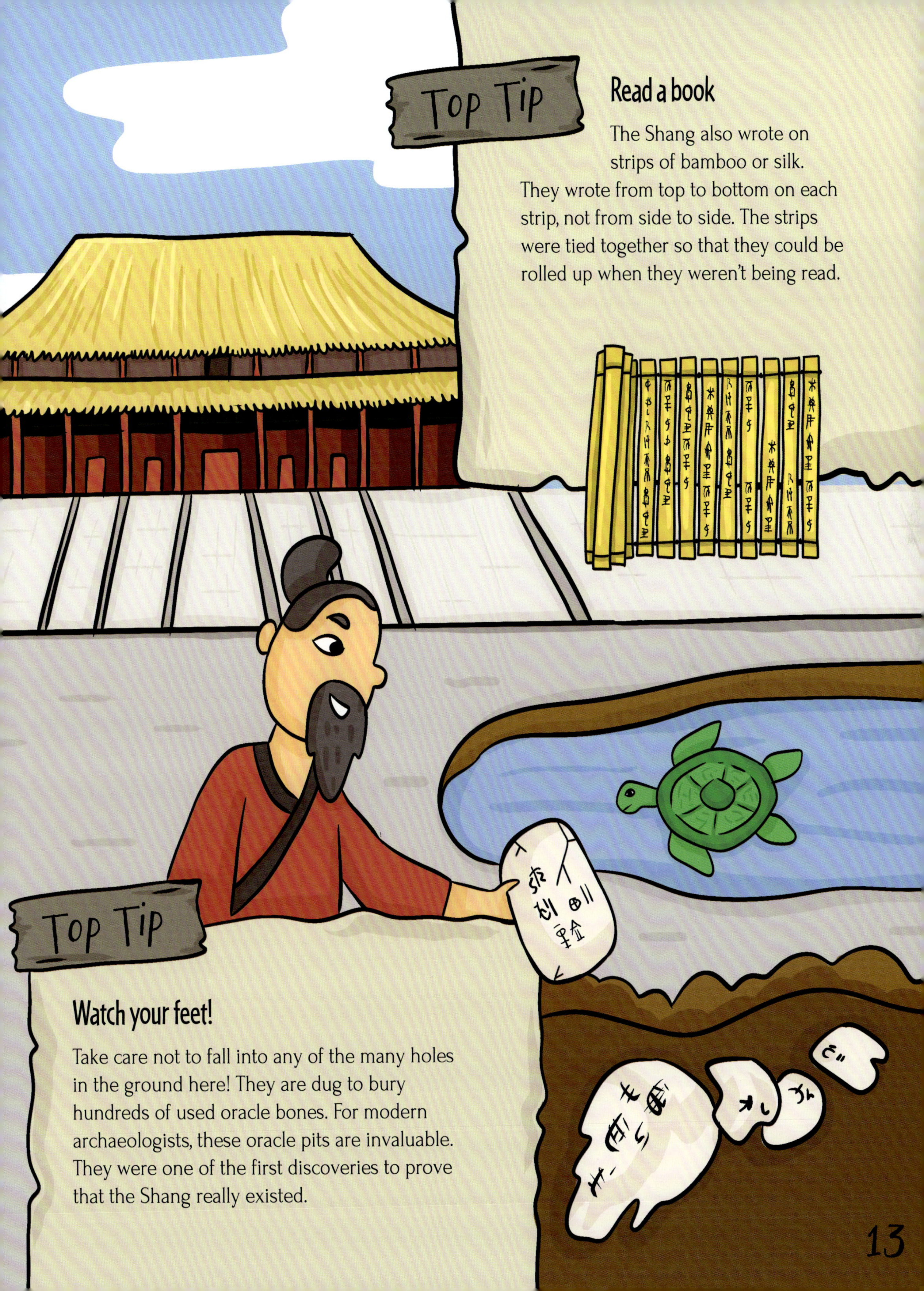

Top Tip

Read a book

The Shang also wrote on strips of bamboo or silk. They wrote from top to bottom on each strip, not from side to side. The strips were tied together so that they could be rolled up when they weren't being read.

Top Tip

Watch your feet!

Take care not to fall into any of the many holes in the ground here! They are dug to bury hundreds of used oracle bones. For modern archaeologists, these oracle pits are invaluable. They were one of the first discoveries to prove that the Shang really existed.

KEEP THE GODS HAPPY

If you don't get to see the king inside his palace, don't be disappointed. Most of the Shang never get to see him, either. But they know he is looking after them. The king's role is to serve as the link between his people and the gods, as well as his subjects' dead ancestors. In total, there will be 30 Shang kings, starting with the founder of the dynasty, Cheng Tang.

Shang Di

Shang Di is the ancestor of all the Shang people and the most important god. Not only do the Shang believe he controls the harvest, weather, and everything in Yin, Shang Di is also said to decide whether Shang kings win in battle. Everyone in Yin believes that keeping Shang Di happy is the key to their good fortune.

A holy calendar

Peek through gaps in the palace walls to spot men wearing long robes. These are priests who carry out different rituals to keep the gods happy. They know when to carry out the rituals by using a calendar. By watching the moon's phases, Shang astronomers have worked out that a year can be divided into 12 months.

Top Tip

Ancestor worship

Before dinner in your host's home, you may be asked to join in a ceremony to honor their ancestors. Food will be placed on a small altar. The Shang believe that their dead ancestors are still around, looking after them. In return, the ancestors must be fed. Often an animal will be sacrificed to feed the ancestors. Some wealthy families may even sacrifice people – usually an enslaved person – to please their ancestors and the gods.

A MUSICAL BREAK

As you walk past the palace buildings, keep your ears open for music. The Shang love music and it is a key part of religious rituals and ceremonies. Special bells are popular, but also look out for bone flutes and panpipes.

Look out for: nao (ritual bells)

Nao are made from the Shang's favorite metal: bronze. They are different sizes and make different sounds. Skilled players combine the sounds to make music in a range of tones. Bronze bells have been found in Shang tombs, because some musicians were buried with their masters in the belief that they would entertain their masters in the afterlife (see page 25).

An ancient orchestra

Musicians also play other instruments, including bronze cymbals and drums. Sadly, no written music has survived since Shang times, so you are lucky to be able to listen to music that nobody has heard for thousands of years.

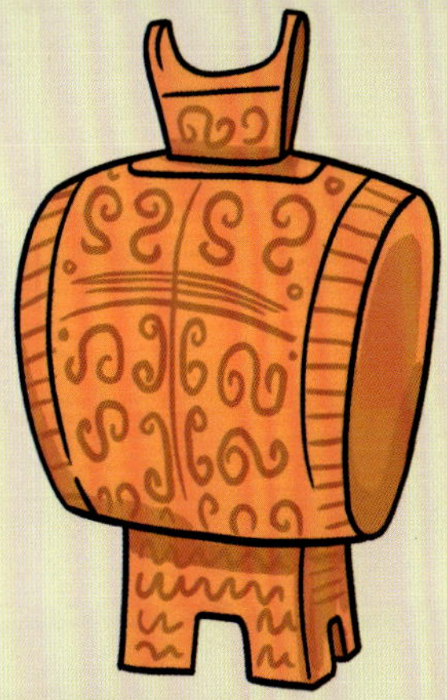

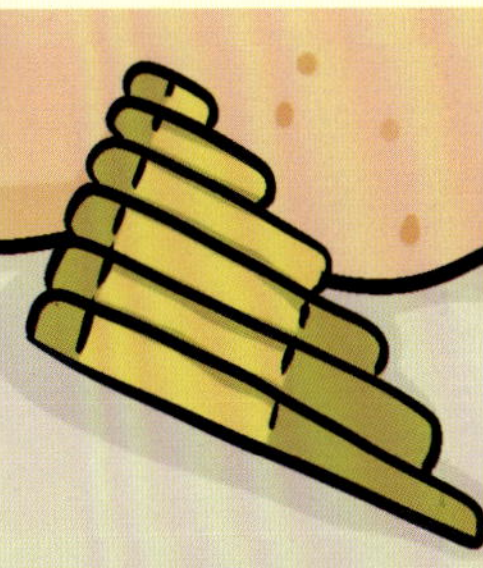

Top Tip

Panpipes

Ask to try some panpipes. These instruments are made from a series of small hollow tubes or pipes, cut into different lengths and tied together in a row. The panpipe player blows air across the holes in the top of the pipes and each pipe makes a different sound.

WHAT'S FOR DINNER?

The Shang eat lots of bread and cheese, and they drink beer. An invitation to a banquet means you will be served more interesting dishes of beans, meat, and fish, and might even lead to the offer of a slice of bear meat!

Time for a banquet

A wealthy customer of your host is holding a banquet. Don't be surprised to learn that this is taking place above their family tomb. It was common to hold banquets in this way, so that the living family could ask the spirits of their ancestors for help. Eat slowly. There may be 20 courses, starting with meat and fish!

Look out for: dings

A *ding* is a special three-legged bronze cooking pot with a lid and two handles. It looks a bit like a large cauldron. Dings are often decorated with complicated designs and unusual shapes. The bigger and more lavish the pot, the richer its owner. You'll find out more about the Shang and bronze later.

A fertile land

Your host has also arranged for you to visit some farms outside the city. You'll travel there in a slow-moving cart pulled by an ox and you'll pass fields full of crops, including millet, barley, and wheat.

When you reach a village, try to spot people using stones to grind grain into flour. They use the flour to make bread. Another very popular dish is congee, a kind of porridge made from millet. Only the royal family and the nobles eat much meat.

Top Tip

Check what you're eating!

It's not unusual for Shang hosts to offer their guests tiger, rhinoceros, or elephant to eat! These rare meats are a special treat. They might be fried with star anise or ginger; both spices can be found in Yin.

TRY WORKING WITH BRONZE

Bronze is the ultimate Shang status symbol. Only the richest and most powerful people own bronze objects. Everyday tools are usually made from stone or wood. Don't miss the chance to visit one of the busy bronze workshops to see amazing craftspeople at work.

How to make bronze objects

Bronze is a mixture of about 80 percent copper and 20 percent tin. The Shang's groundbreaking technology is called piece-mold casting. In the past, people worked metal by hammering it into shape. The Shang found out how to melt bronze and tip it into molds to make complex shapes.

First, they make a clay mold of the design. Then, they heat bronze until it melts. The liquid bronze is poured into the mold and left to cool. Once it has hardened, the mold is cracked open to reveal the bronze item inside. Bronze tools were then sharpened by rubbing a stone along the blade.

Top Tip

Stand back!

When the craftspeople pour the liquid bronze into the mold, make sure you stay at a safe distance. Molten metal is very hot!

Look out for: the taotie

If you look at the sides of some bronze vessels, you might be in for a shock! Some have a face with bulging eyes, horns, a snout, and fangs. Some historians think that this is the face of an evil spirit called a *taotie*, one of the four worst monsters in Chinese mythology.

DRESS LIKE A LOCAL

If you want to dress like the Shang, look at the elite who set the style in Yin. They dress in silk robes and wear beautiful jewelry. The Shang check how they look before they leave their homes. Every rich household has a mirror of polished bronze, so they can see themselves.

A shared wardrobe

Wealthy Shang men and women dress in similar silk robes. Women and men alike coil their hair and use carved bone hairpins to secure it in a bun. Both men and women have pierced ears, so they can wear earrings.

Look out for: silk

The Shang adore silk. It's light, smooth, cool to wear in the summer and warm in winter. According to legend, Xi Ling-shi, the wife of the legendary Yellow Emperor, Huangdi, discovered silk in 3000 BCE, long before the Shang existed. She invented a loom on which silk could be woven, after seeing a silk moth fall into water and release its silk threads.

Look out for: jade

Much of the jewelry worn by people in Yin is made from a semi-precious stone called jade. They wear necklaces of jade beads, bracelets, rings, earrings, hair combs, and brooches. They even use hooks to hang jade objects from their belts. The Shang love jade!

A ROYAL TOMB

Ask your host to arrange a trip to visit the royal cemetery and tombs. It's not far, so you can probably walk. One of the tombs is now the most famous of all Shang sites. It belonged to a queen called Fu Hao.

Fu Hao

Fu Hao was the favorite of the 64 wives of King Wu Ding, and the greatest Shang general of her time. She was a formidable warrior and led the Shang army into battle to defeat their enemies. Fu Hao owned lots of land, which made her even more important.

When she died, Wu Ding gave her a grand funeral and tomb, which is located just outside the royal cemetery. Grave robbers never found her tomb, which is why many of its treasures remain today.

Visitors to modern Yinxu (see page 29) can also see a statue of Fu Hao close to her tomb!

Look out for: grave goods

A Shang tomb is packed full of objects the dead person used while they were alive. Inside her grave, Fu Hao was buried with six dogs, 16 servants, 564 pieces of bone (shaped into, for example, arrowheads and hairpins), 755 pieces of jade, more than 400 pieces of bronze, including weapons and bells ... and 6,900 cowrie shells (see page 27) to use as money to buy goods in the afterlife!

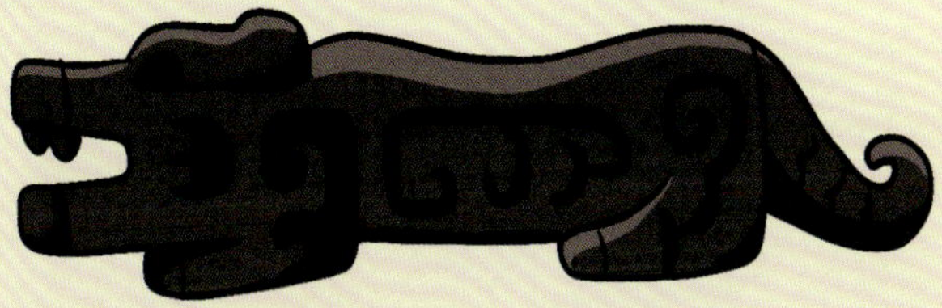

Look out for: weapons

Bronze is so prized that elite warriors like Fu Hao were buried with their bronze axes, swords, daggers, and helmets. Fu Hao was even buried with her horses and chariot!

TIME TO SHOP

A time traveler will want some souvenirs of their visit. For the best choice, head out of town to where the markets are held. That's where most shops are also found. Nearly all the goods on offer are things the Shang make themselves.

Fit for a king

The best goods are snapped up by the royal family. They buy most of the silk that's produced. If you do see silk for sale, then buy it! Shang silk is of fantastic quality.

Look out for: jade dragons

Jade is so hard that it can only be shaped by slowly grinding it with wet sand. That takes a long time and explains why jade is so precious. As well as using jade for jewelry, the Shang carve jade dragons – these make great presents. The Shang believe that dragons are kind animals that protect everyone and provide help when needed. Many Shang buildings have carvings of dragons on the roof to protect the building and the people inside.

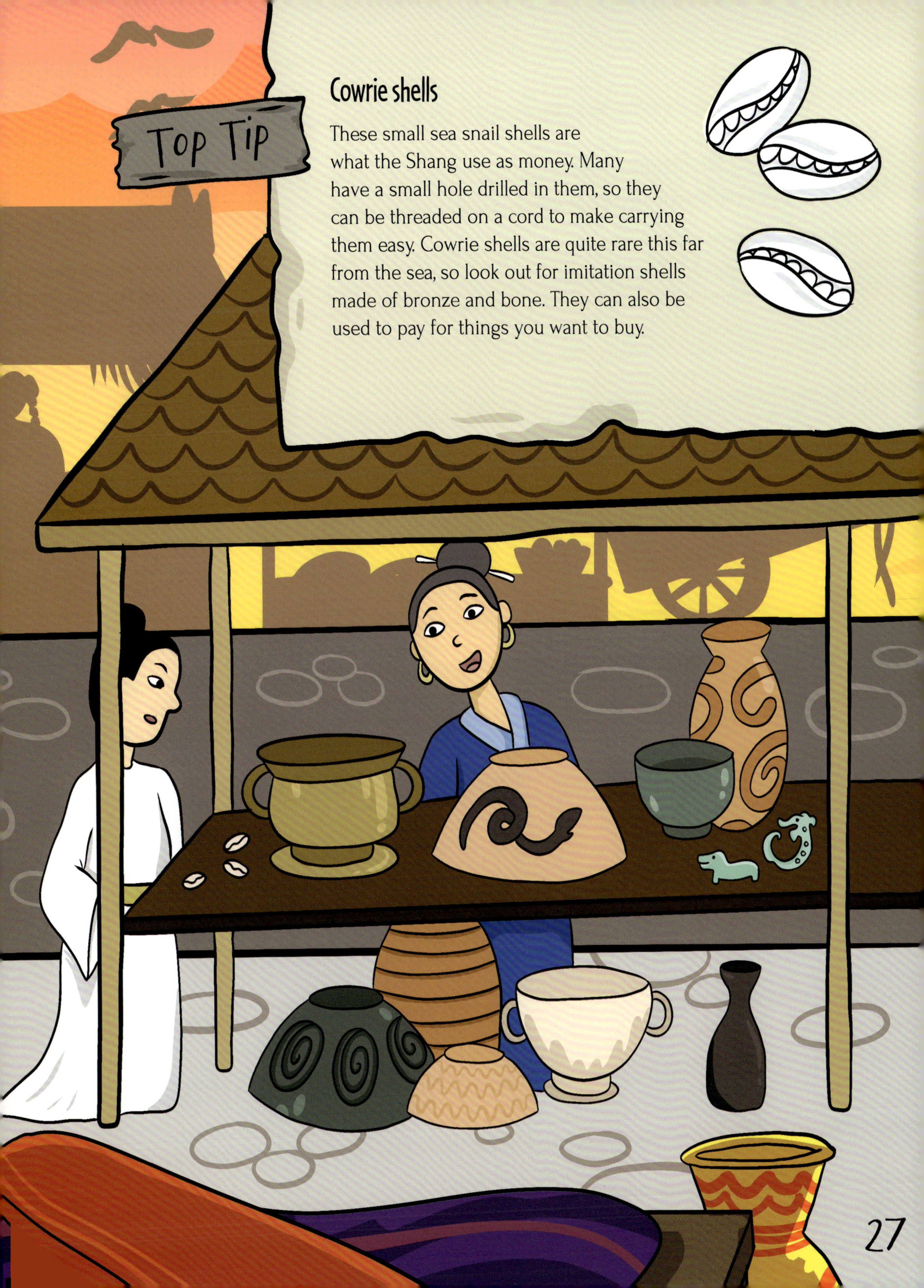

Top Tip

Cowrie shells

These small sea snail shells are what the Shang use as money. Many have a small hole drilled in them, so they can be threaded on a cord to make carrying them easy. Cowrie shells are quite rare this far from the sea, so look out for imitation shells made of bronze and bone. They can also be used to pay for things you want to buy.

VISIT QUICK!

Life is good under the Shang, and Yin is a fascinating place to visit but, sadly, that won't last forever. After more than 500 years of peaceful rule, the Shang Dynasty will eventually come to an end as they are defeated by their enemies, the Zhou.

The Shang Dynasty ends

Around 1122 BCE, the Zhou Dynasty was founded on the edge of the Shang Dynasty's lands. To begin with, that was not a problem. The two dynasties lived peacefully side by side. But Di Xin, the last Shang ruler, treated his people badly.

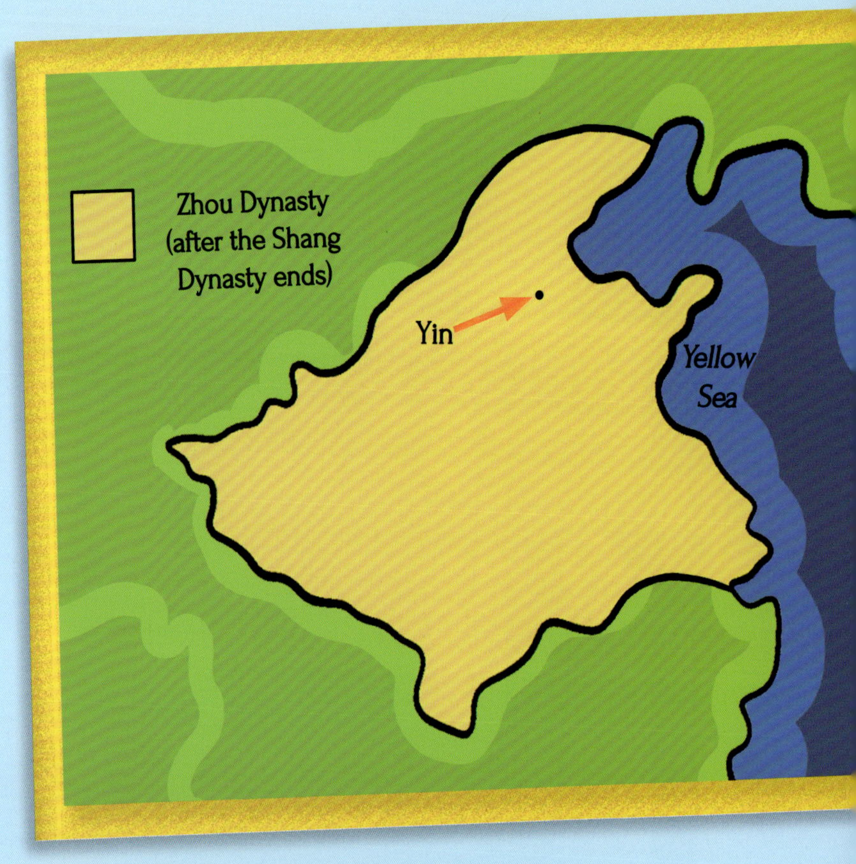

Di Xin

The Zhou Dynasty begins

In 1046 BCE, the Zhou army marched on Yin. Di Xin tried to get 200,000 enslaved people to help his army defend the city. But many soldiers and enslaved people refused to fight for him. Some even joined the Zhou forces. Di Xin killed himself and the Zhou took charge.

The legacy of the Shang

The Shang Dynasty lasted for only about 550 years, but it changed Chinese history. To find out how, you're going to need to time travel again. This time, you should visit Yinxu (as it is then called) in the late 1920s, when archaeologists started to explore its ruins. Yinxu translates from Chinese as "ruins of Yin."

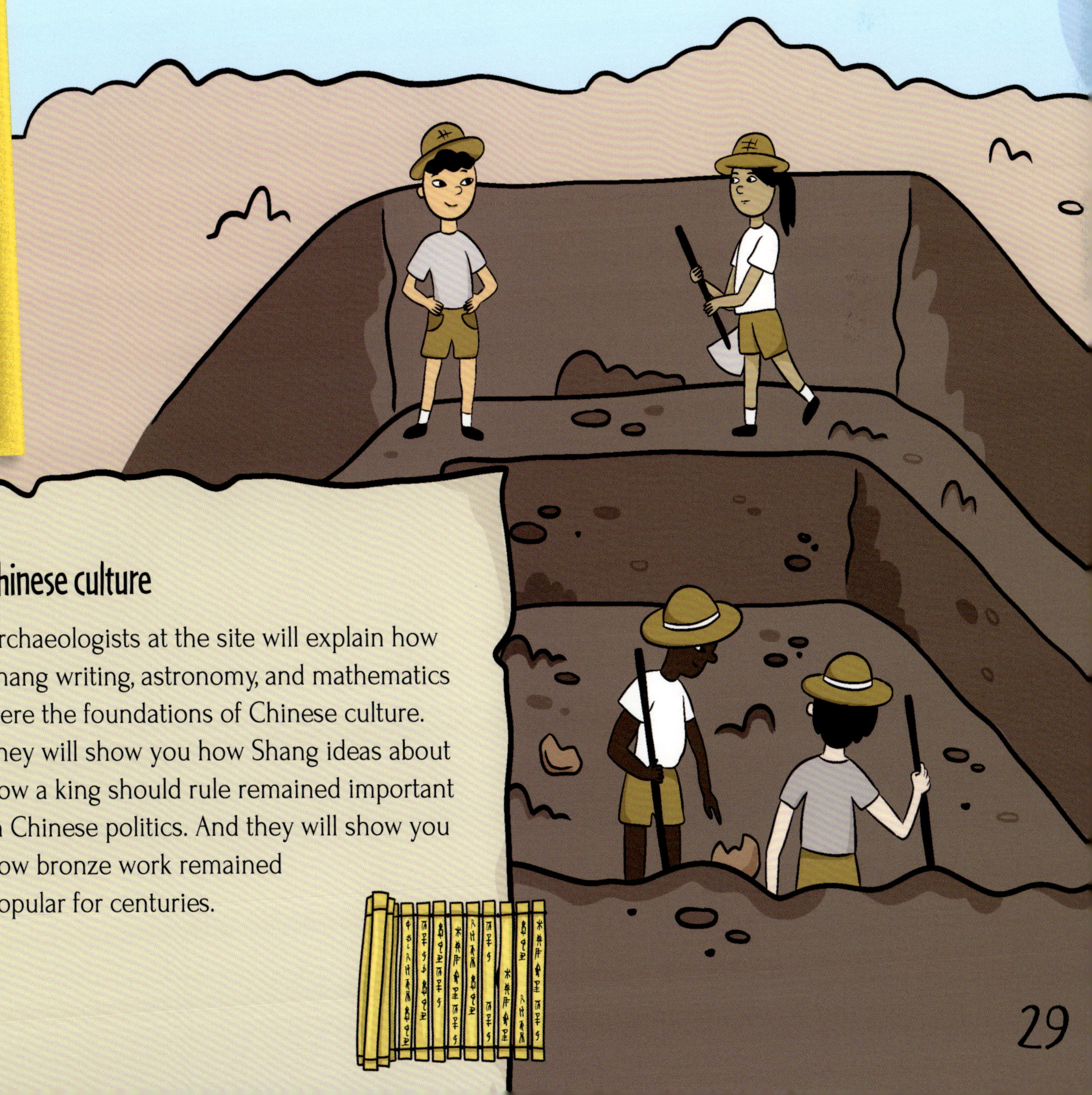

Chinese culture

Archaeologists at the site will explain how Shang writing, astronomy, and mathematics were the foundations of Chinese culture. They will show you how Shang ideas about how a king should rule remained important in Chinese politics. And they will show you how bronze work remained popular for centuries.

GLOSSARY

Altar A flat stone or table used for religious worship.

Ancestor A member of someone's family who lived long ago, usually before their grandparents.

Archaeologist Someone who studies history by examining objects, buildings, and ruins from the past.

Bronze A golden-brown metal that is an alloy of copper and tin. An alloy is a mixture of two or more metals.

Ceremony An event that celebrates something, such as an achievement, anniversary, or religious occasion.

Chinese mythology Stories told in ancient China about gods, goddesses, and the origins of the world.

Formidable Describing someone who is powerful and impressive at something, such as fighting or leading an army.

Imitation A copy of the real thing.

Loom A wooden frame used to weave cloth.

Luxurious Describing a very comfortable lifestyle, often with great wealth and many expensive and beautiful things.

Merchant Someone who buys and sells goods, often transporting them to markets.

Moon's phases The way the moon appears to change shape each month, from a full moon to a crescent moon to a half moon and back again.

Oxen Adult male cows that are used for meat or as a work animal.

Ritual An act or set of actions that is performed in a particular way, usually as part of a religious ceremony.

Sacrifice To make an offering of something valuable, for example food to a god.

Star anise A small, dried, brown, star-shaped fruit with seeds inside it. Star anise has an aniseed-like flavor and is often used as a spice in Asian cooking.

Thatch A roof made of straw.

Tomb A grave or building that is used to hold a dead body.

Tone The pitch (highness or lowness) and sound of a musical note.

FURTHER INFORMATION

Books

A Question of History: Why Did the Shang Write on Turtles?
Tim Cooke (Wayland, 2022)

Uncover History: Shang Dynasty
Geoff Barker (Wayland, 2023)

Websites

Discover more facts and information about all things Shang at:
kids.britannica.com/kids/article/Shang-dynasty/353765/

For lots of information on the Shang, visit this BBC bitesize website:
www.bbc.co.uk/bitesize/topics/z39j2hv

To find more information about the Shang Dynasty, visit:
www.ks2history.com/shang-dynasty-guide

INDEX